Red or Blue?

Written by Jenni Stevens Illustrated by Pamela R. Levy

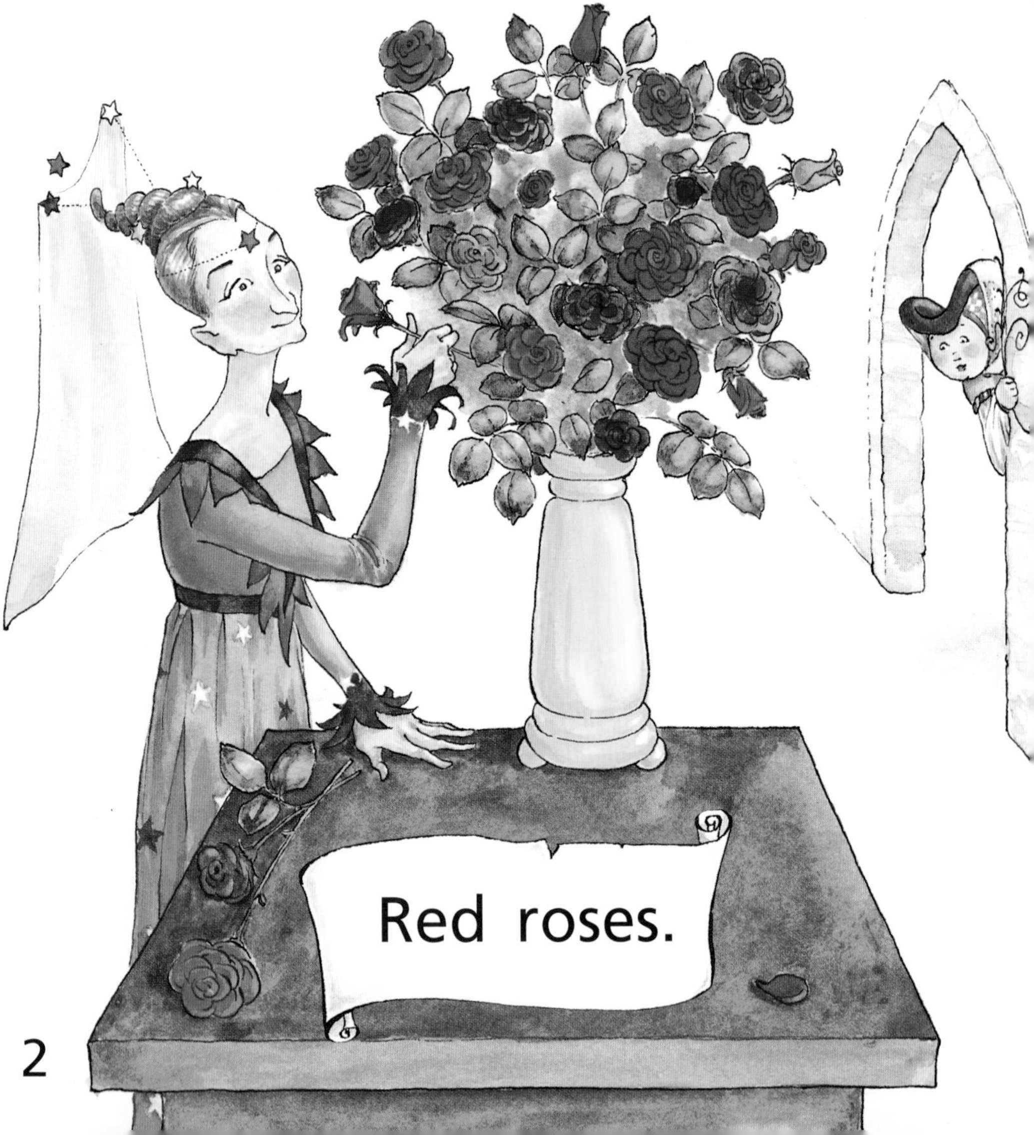
Red roses.

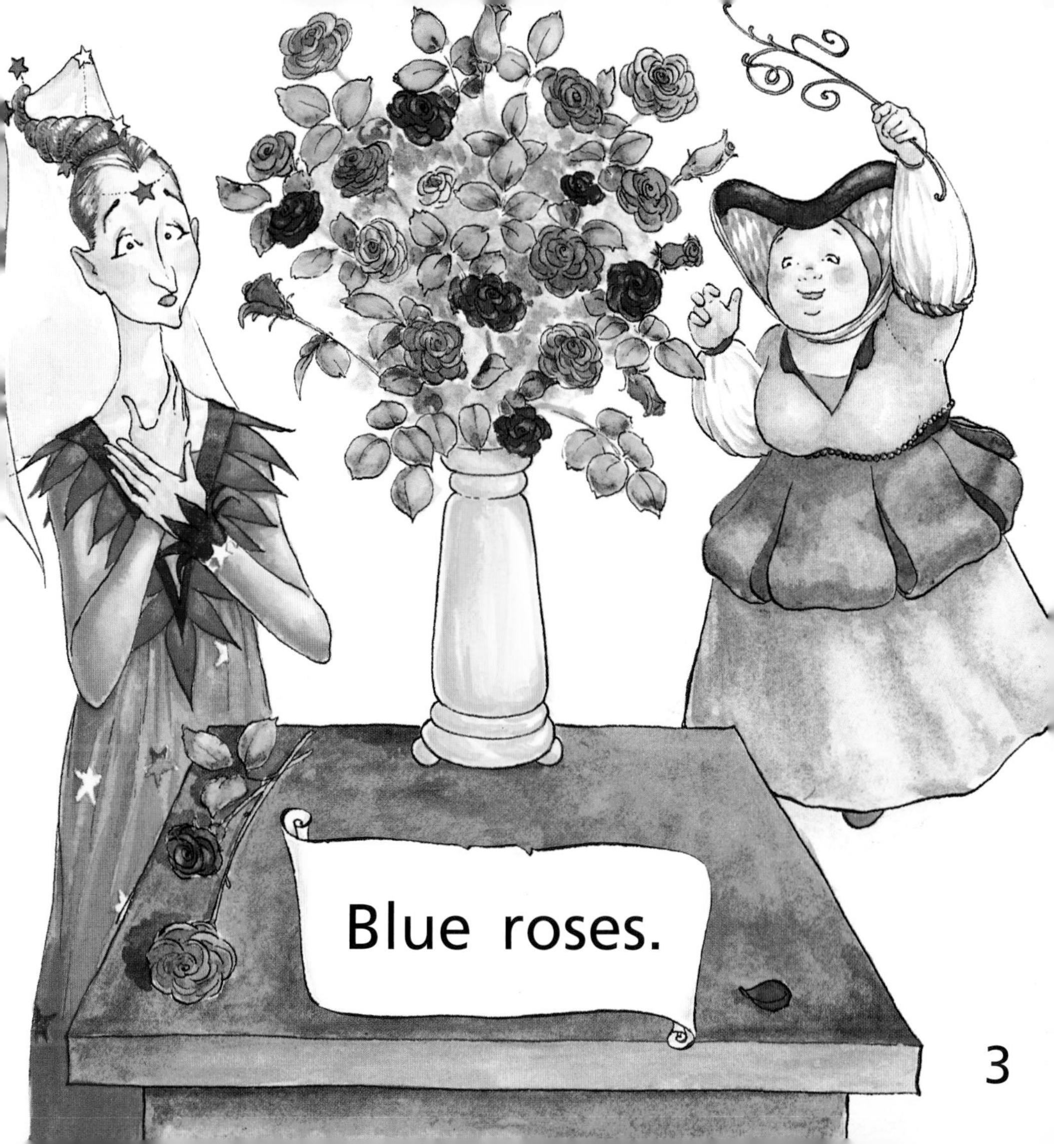
Blue roses.

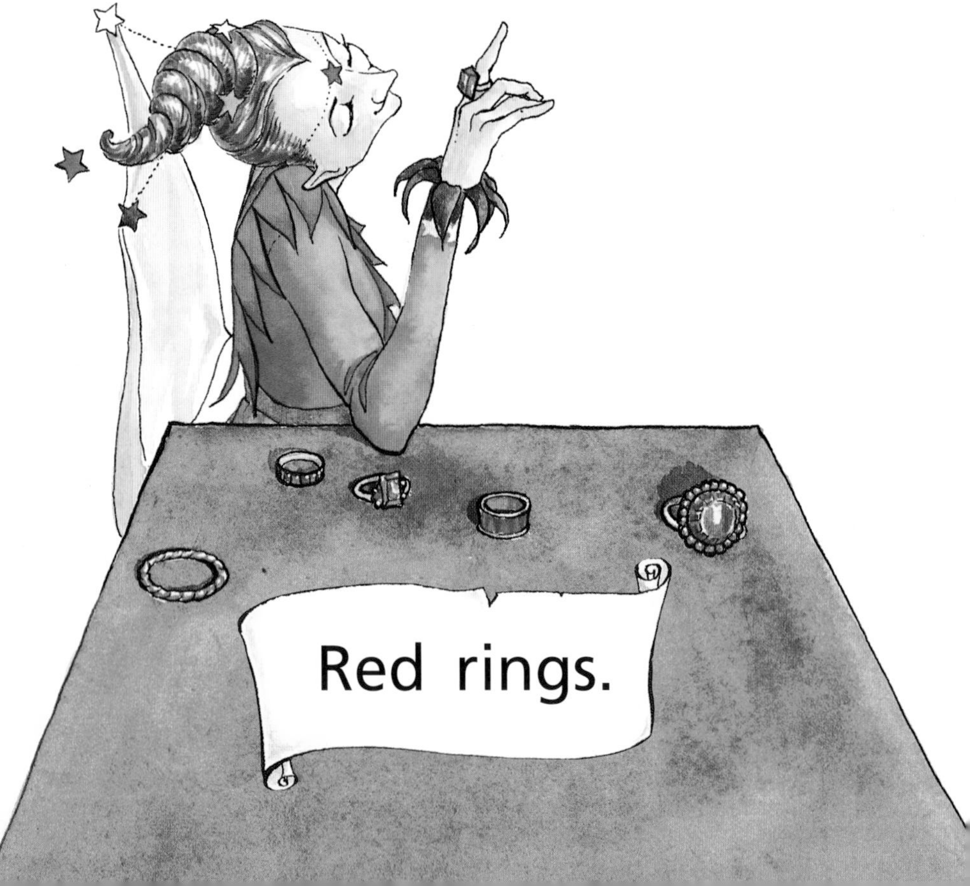
Red rings.

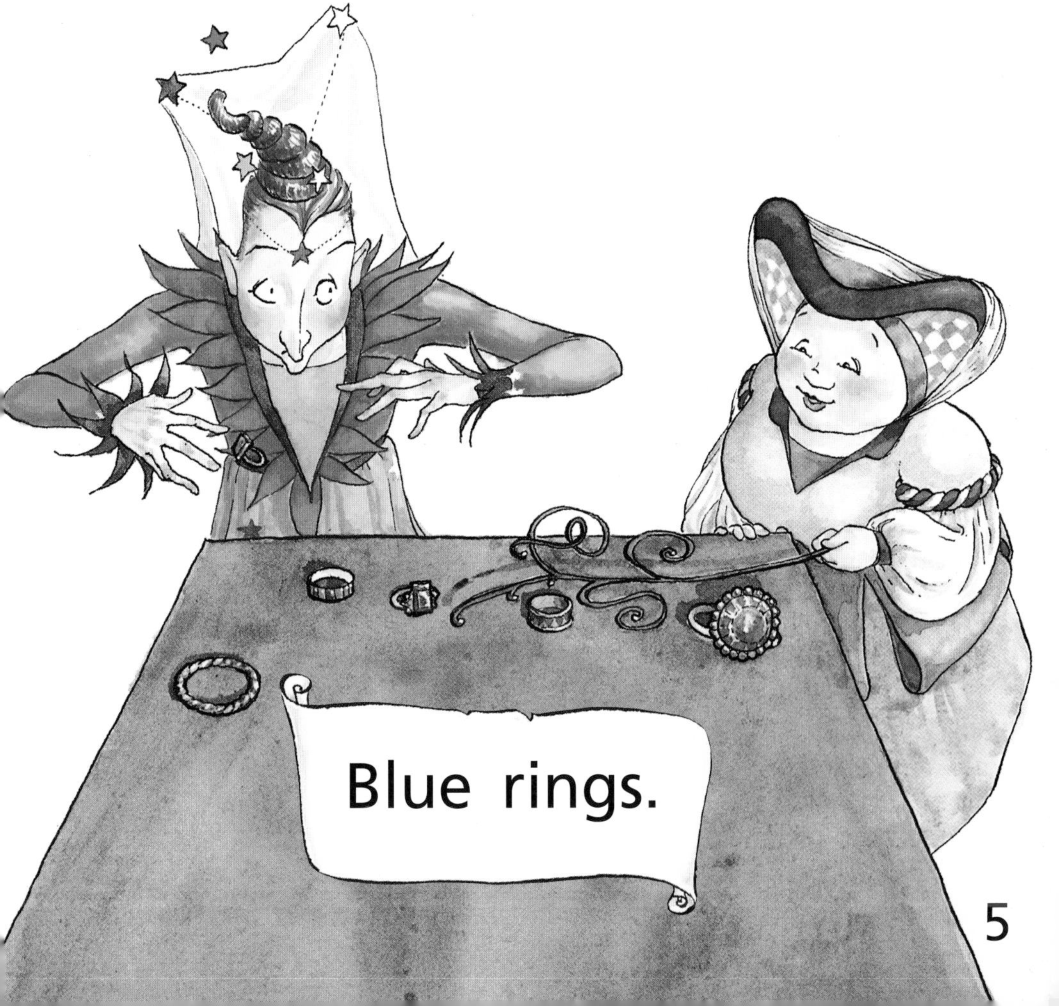

Blue rings.

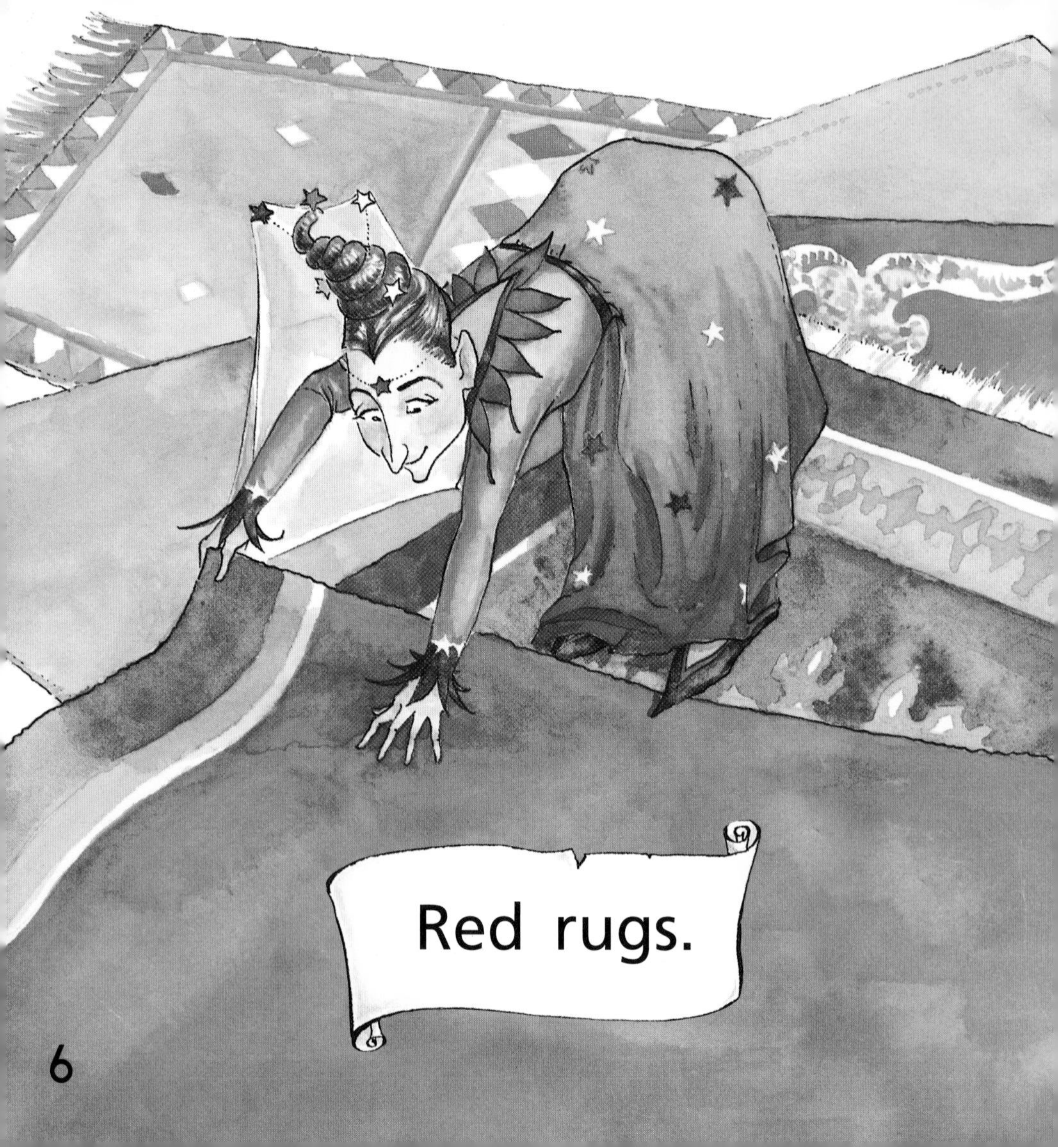

Red rugs.

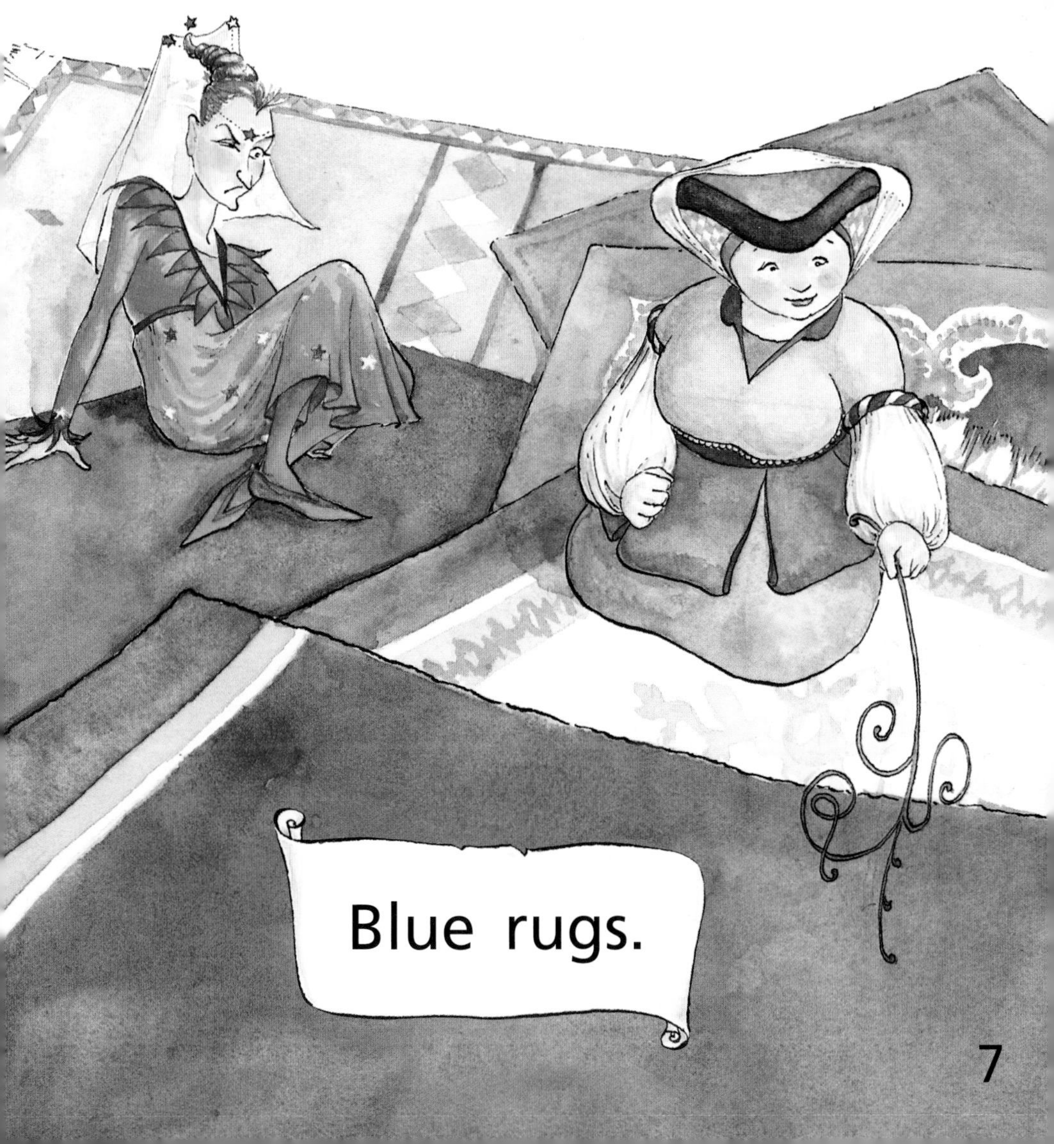

Blue rugs.

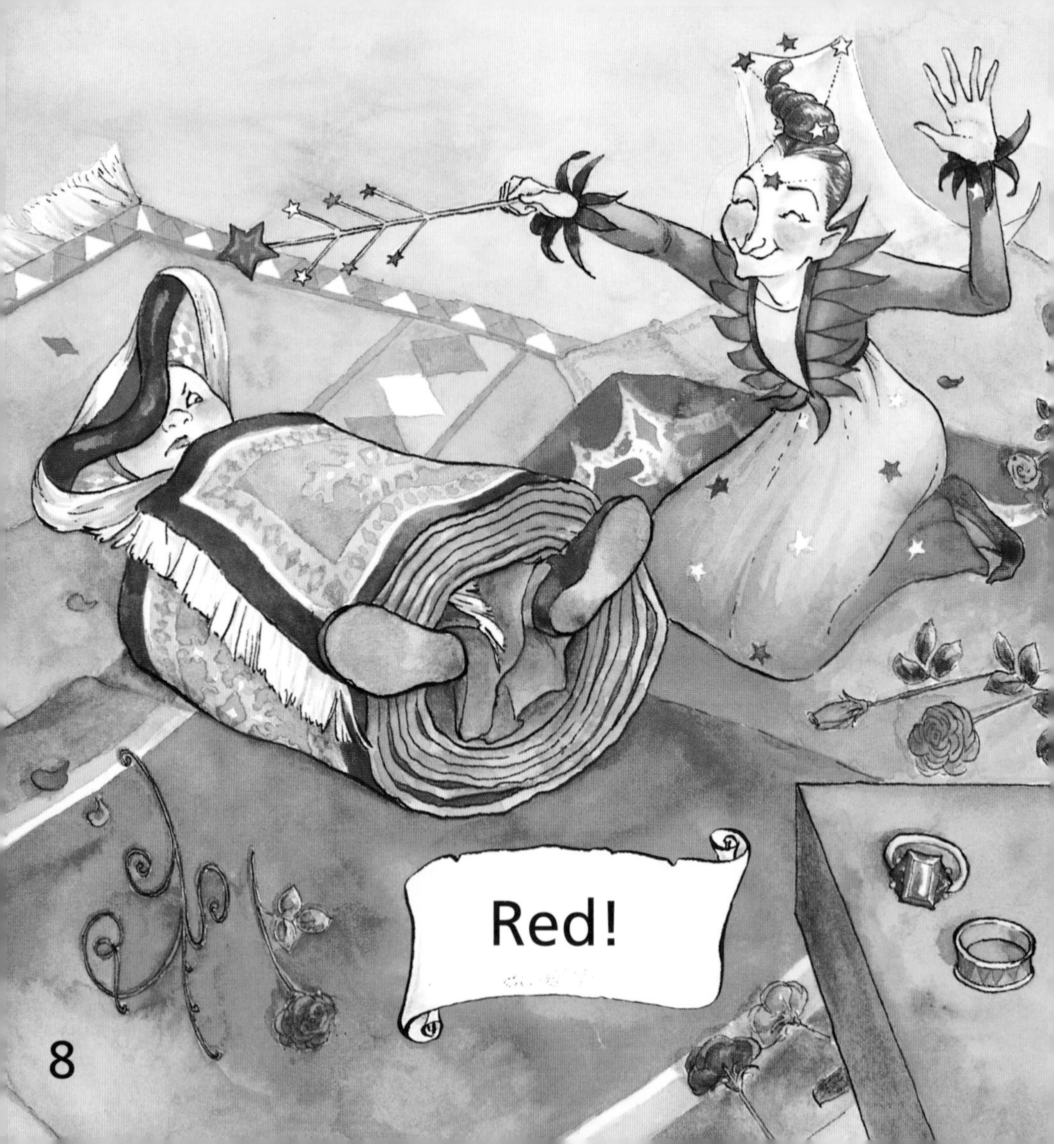
Red!